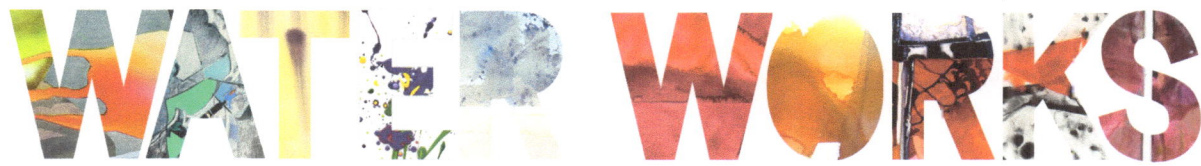

July 5 - August 17, 2014   THE PORCH GALLERY - OJAI, CALIFORNIA

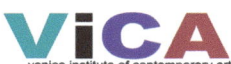
venice institute of contemporary art

Water Works
July 5 - August 17, 2014
Porch Gallery, Ojai, California

Produced by
Venice Institute of Contemporary Art
Porch Gallery, Ojai, California

The catalogue production has been
supported in part by the Sam Francis
Foundation, California

www.veniceica.org
www.porchgalleryojai.com
www.samfrancisfoundation.org

Special Thanks
Lisa Casoni, Heather Stobo,
Peter Frank, Shana Nys Dambrot,
John Seed, Debra Burchett-Lere
Nancy Escher, Wendy Elliott

Graphic Design
Heather Stobo
Juri Koll

Available from Amazon.com and other book stores

ISBN-13:
978-0692237229 (Venice Institute of Contemporary Art)

ISBN-10:
0692237224

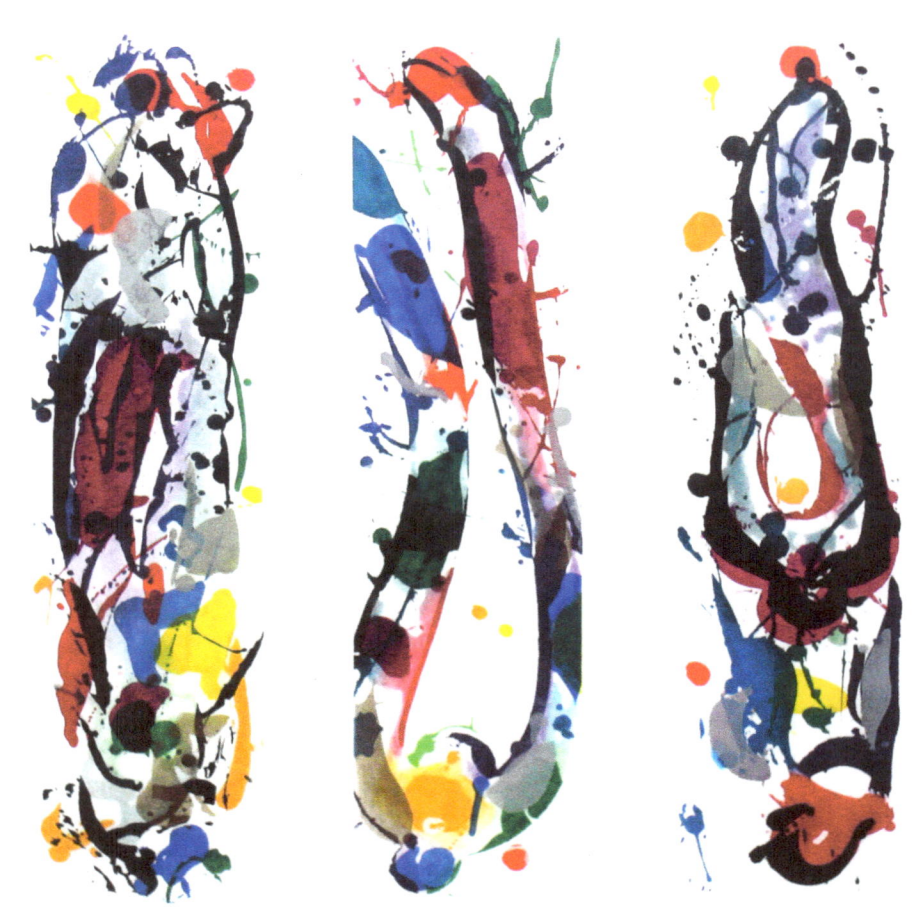

Sam Francis
Untitled, 1987 aquatint (edition of 20) 36 x 32 1/8 inches
On Loan from the Collection of Wendy Elliott

One day in 1977 I was an art student in the waiting area of the Oakland airport when I realized that the man sitting next to me was Sam Francis. I struck up a conversation and we made small talk until I told Sam that when I got to Los Angeles I was going to see a dermatologist: my hands were dry and wrecked from the oil paints, solvents and harsh soaps that I was using at the time.

Once he saw my hands Francis gave me a lecture and I listened. He told me that he had dealt with many illnesses related to artist's materials and that he had switched to acrylic partly because of his concerns over solvents. He told me in a fatherly tone that I needed to wear gloves, be very careful around paint and consider switching to water-based acrylics.

Six years later the art dealer Riko Mizuno asked me: "Do you want to meet Sam?" I jumped at the chance to see him again, but when we got to Francis' Santa Monica studio he wasn't there. However, the place made a big impression on me even without its impresario. The spattered floor tarps, color-speckled walls and brilliantly-hued paintings leaning against them told stories of energetic ebbs and flows. There wasn't a whiff of turpentine in the place.

Fast-forwarding to now I am so very honored to be a member of the board of the Sam Francis Foundation, and to see Sam's work exhibited in the exhibition "Water Works." He truly understood the value of water: it is a universal solvent, an essential force of nature, and a source of health.

John Seed - June, 2014

CRY ME A RIVER: WATER WORKS AS ART

Depictions of liquids, of fluidity, seem almost contradictory. How can you fix an image of something that by nature is quixotic, constantly changing? You go with the flow. That is to say, you accept the Heisenbergian principle that your rendition will be a brute approximation of the real thing, that whether you seek to depict a rush of water or capitalize on its physical effects, you can't get it quite right, so you get it as right as you can.

The materials employed in the production of two-dimensional artwork can be characterized as wet or dry. Handily enough, that's a good way of dividing our perceptual experience of the world. Of course, in art as in the world, the condition of things gradates between the dry and set and the humid and mutable. But at a certain point, gradations of fluency escape our perception. Is cascading water wetter than oozing? Is water itself wetter than oil? Where does acrylic, or gouache, fall in this liquefactive scale? (And what about quicksand?)

Some of the artworks gathered here show wateriness; others embody it. Some of the works rely on media that flow slower than what they are made to depict, while others seem barely to keep up with the rush of their own imagery. All, however, evoke a wetness, no matter how viscous, a readiness to trickle or to gush, to define form as the effect of gravity on mercurial material. They go with the flow. There is a justice - not just poetic, but visceral - that work by Sam Francis anchors the show and in essence reveals him as its paterfamilias fluidus: Francis' entire oeuvre was, if anything, an extended virtuosic exploration of aqueousness.

The effects of water fascinated artists for centuries. In the last several decades, the effect of water itself has been a powerful spur to experiment. The drip, the stain, the cloud, the leaked tendril, all these and many more formations became standard in the vocabulary of late modernism, and the painters, watercolorists, even printmakers and photographers of today work in the efflux of their predecessors' practices. We have gone from wading through veritable waterfalls looking for signs and dreams, as the abstract expressionists did, to allowing the waterfalls themselves to define the shape and feel of the artworks before us. Meaning has shifted from imagination to sensation, a historical arc that links surrealism to process art and earthworks. But sensation, in turn, provokes imagination; just as clouds suggest images, images themselves - the images in artworks, no matter how accidental or sensual - conjure nebulous infinities. It is not up to us to interpret what stands- or, you might say, flows - by us but to comprehend it all as phenomena capable of working upon us.

Where does it work upon us? Not on the leg or the spleen, but on the eye, and thus directly on the brain. Art's basic flow courses between human mind and material, and then between object and human mind. If the mind itself is a river, the materials of art are the stones it shapes and the fish it hosts, the flotsam it carries and the banks it laps. All art is wet.

Peter Frank - June 2014

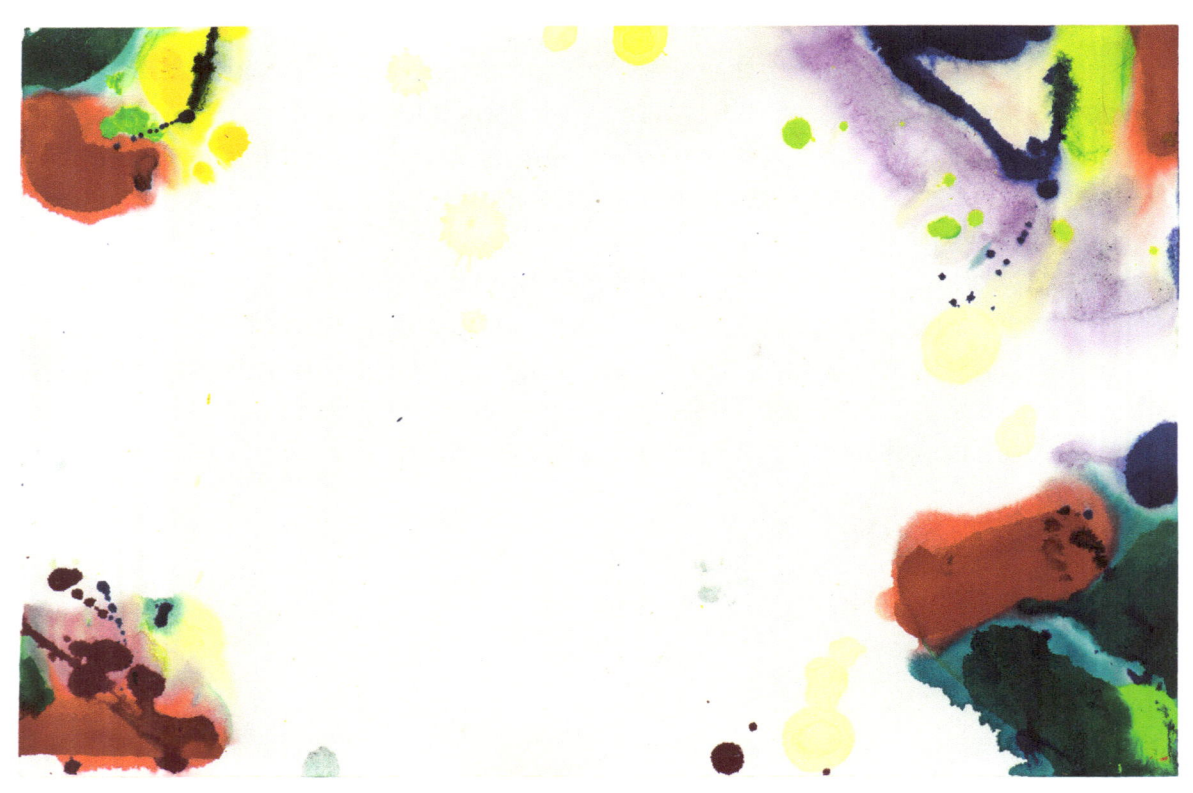

Sam Francis
Untitled, 1968
Acrylic on paper 12 x 18 inches
On loan from the private collection of Nancy Escher, Ojai, CA

"Water is another matter, it has no direction but its own bright grace..."
Pablo Neruda

Water is an emblem of fluidity in the material world. In dream analysis, water is a common Jungian metaphor for the subconscious mind. Its various naturally occurring and familiar manmade forms - rivers, lakes, oceans; rain, dew, puddles; swimming pools, faucets, fountains; waterfalls, brooks, tall cold glasses to drink - and its various states of calm, agitation, storminess, damming-up; cleanliness, darkness, dirtiness, purity; scarcity, gentleness, power, depth, and danger indicate a range of emotions from fear to fertility, inspiration, exuberance, soaring serenity, and existential unrest. In a dream, these factors reveal an understanding of one's basic state of being. Watercolor paint is a little like that, too.

Water-based paints, inks, and dyes find their level, following water's laws which despite the pigments' duties as studio materials are in fact the laws of nature. Direct, immediate, nuanced, and responsive to the artist's hand, water-based mediums defy attempts at revision, demanding that the artist work quickly and intuitively, and be acutely present in the moment. These Water-Workers deploy their materials in a diverse array of styles; some embrace the chaos, some set themselves a challenge of directing it. But all are drawn to water's ineluctably lively physicality; and all have made their peace with getting wet and messy.

Shana Nys Dambrot - June 2014

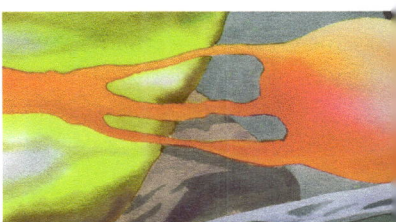

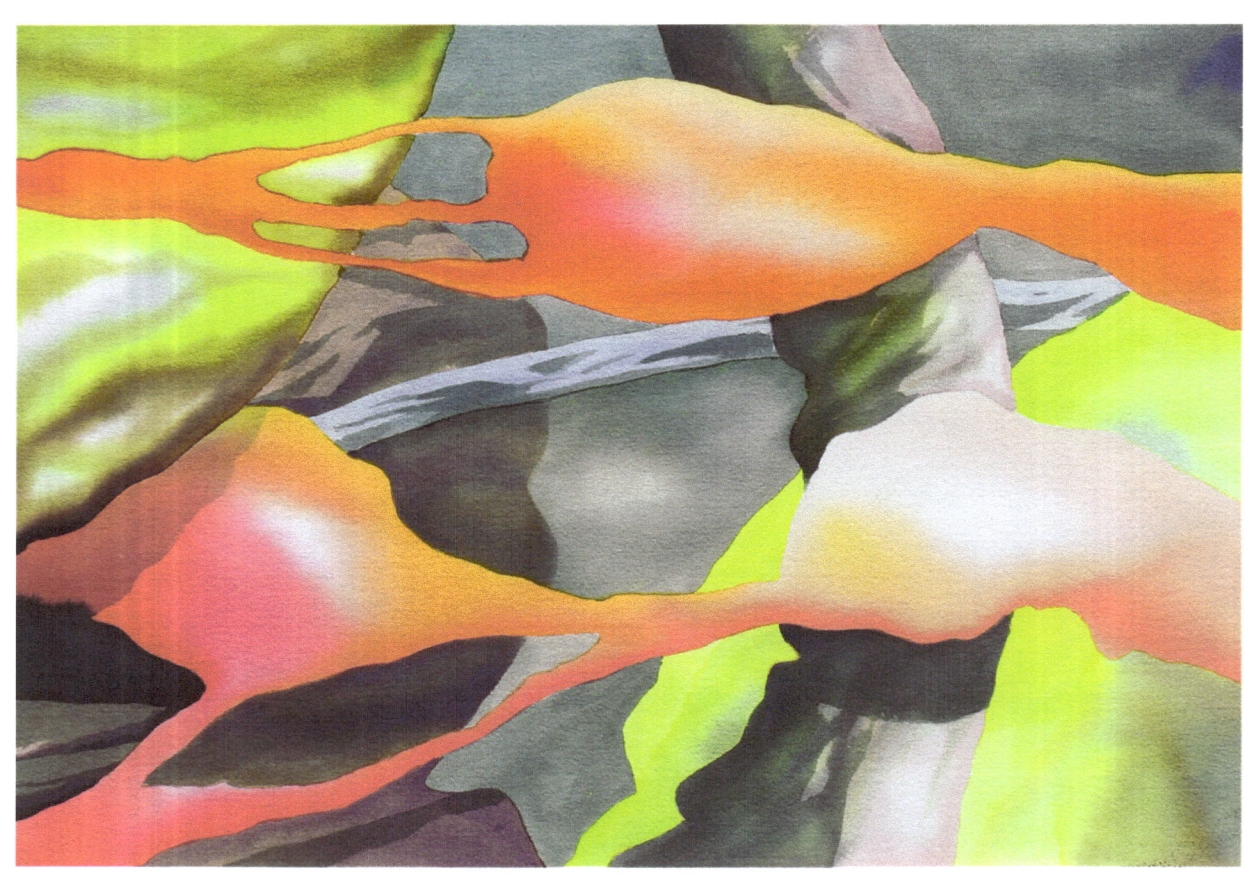

The Dark Bob
Untitled, 2010
Watercolor on Arches Paper, 16 X 20 inches

THE DARK BOB

Born in Santa Monica, California, The Dark Bob began his performance art career in 1975 when he cofounded the multimedia art team of Bob & Bob. This early work has been historicized in books, catalogs and documentary profiles for television, radio and film. He is generally regarded as a pioneer in L.A. performance art.

His one-man multimedia shows combine song, dance, film, storytelling, live onstage painting and comedy. The Dark Bob's artworks (drawings, paintings, sculptures and installations) have been exhibited in galleries and museums across America and around the world.

He has been featured on numerous local television shows around the U.S. and has appeared many times on radio stations in this country and abroad: "Life & Time Tonight", KCETPBS TV profile, "California Stories", KCETPBS TV profile, NPR (National Public Radio) profile by Elizabeth Perez Luna, "Views From L.A", by MVC TV, "Young Turks", a documentary film by Stephen Seemayer, The Pacifica Radio National Network Interview, "The Territory of Art" produced by The Museum of Contemporary Art (Los Angeles), and others. He is currently working on a new documentary with ViCA.

A multitude profiles, articles and reviews have been written on The Dark Bob, notably: The Washington Post, The Los Angeles Times, Village Voice, L.A. Weekly, The Chicago Reader, Artforum and Artweek.

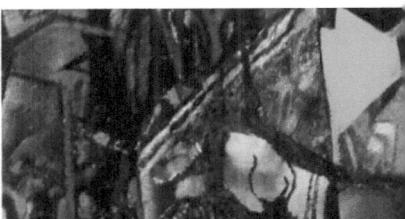

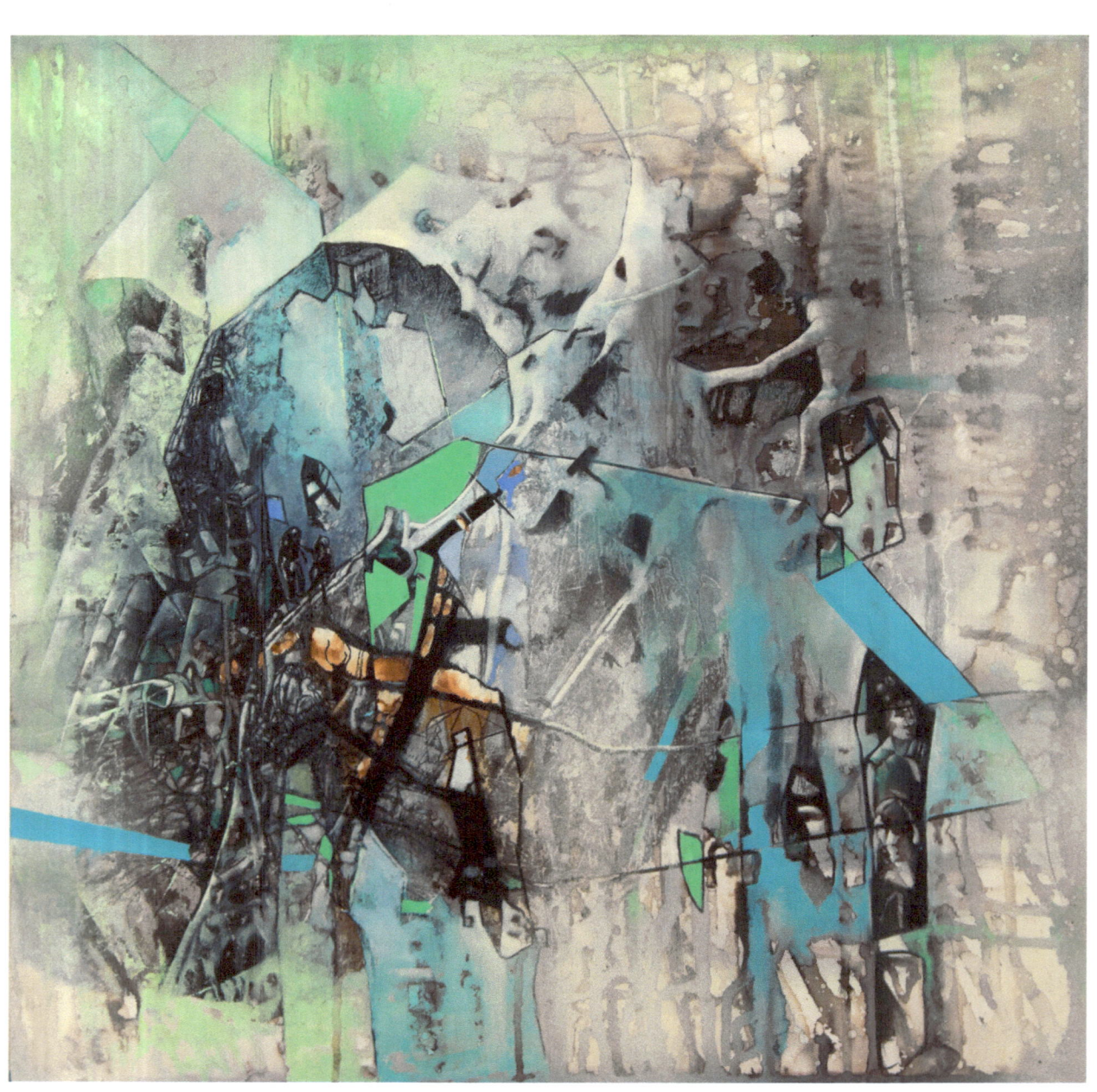

Fatemeh Burnes
Chamber, 2014
Oil and Prismacolor on paper mounted to panel, 16 x 16 inches

FATEMEH BURNES

Fatemeh Burnes was born in Tehran. She first came to the United States in 1973, spent a five-year period between three continents, and settled in Southern Californiain 1977. Classically trained in Persian art and verse, Burnes also studied biology, and western artistic practice - including painting, drawing, printmaking, photography, art history, and exhibition design - in Iran, Europe, and ultimately in California, where she received her BFA and MFA in art and art history.

Burnes has taught fine arts, design, and art history at California State University Fullerton, the Art Institute of Southern California (now the Laguna College of Art and Design), and several other colleges.

Since 1992 Burnes has served as gallery director and curator as well as full-time professor of drawing and design at Mt. San Antonio College. She has curated over 100 exhibitions, authored numerous publications, conducted art-education documentaries, and worked with an international array of artists and art professionals. She has exhibited her own work extensively since the 1980s.

Since re-emerging in 2009 with new bodies of work in painting and photography, Burnes has earned the attention of top critics and curators in Southern California and has gained national and international recognition. In January 2012 Zero+ Publishing released drift, a book of Burnes' photographs, edited by critic and writer Peter Frank and in March 2013 she published a 220-page full-color catalogue, Imprints of Nature and Human Nature, to accompany a solo exhibition at Mt. San Antonio College. She has also exhibited at the Municipal Arts Gallery in Los Angeles among many other venues, and her exhibitions have been reviewed in publications such as art ltd, ArtScene, and the Huffington Post.

In 2014 Burnes is featured "Trans-Angeles," a traveling exhibition curated by Peter Frank which opened the Wilhelm-Morgner-Haus in Soest, Germany.

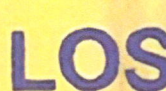

LOS

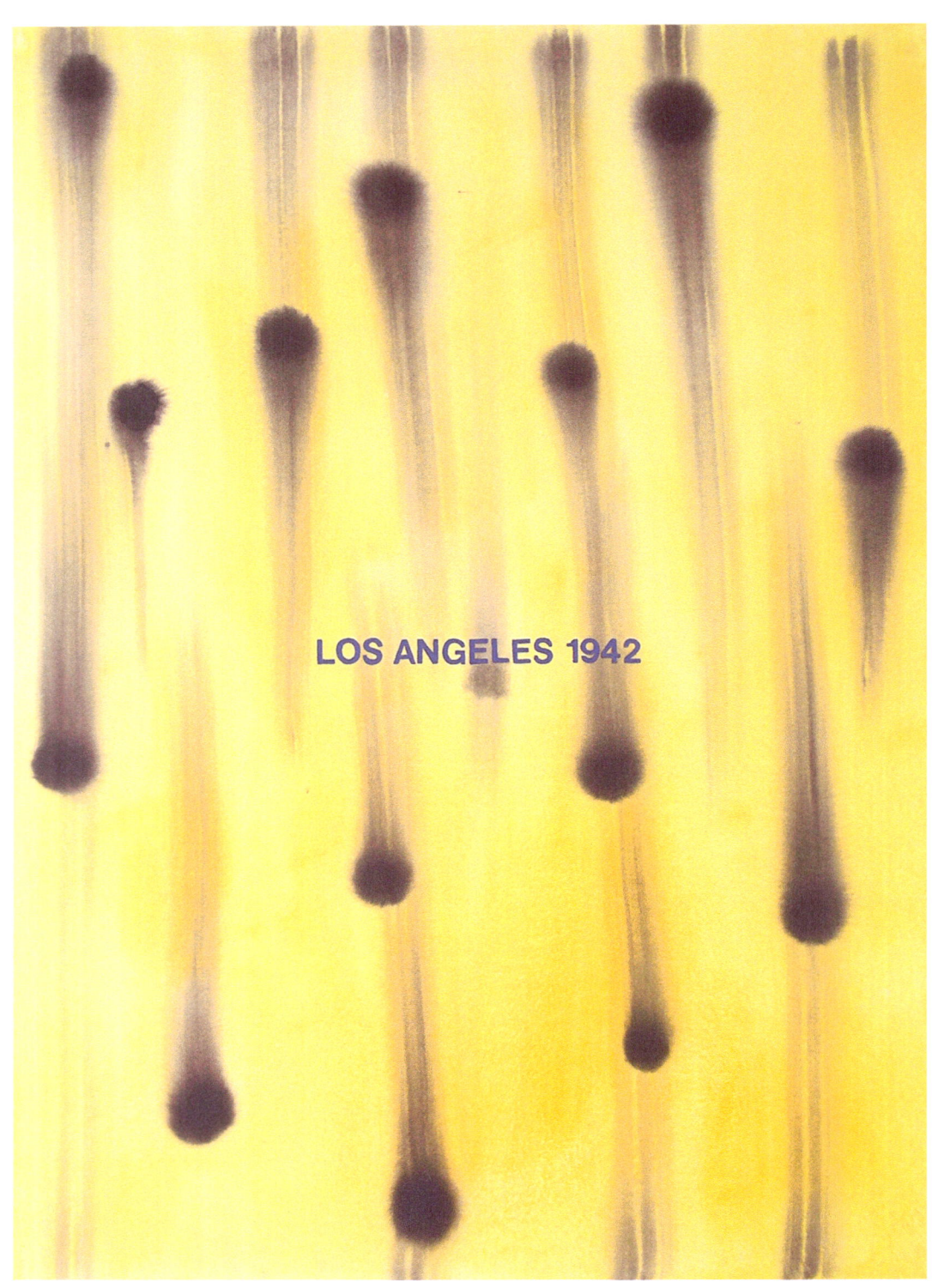

Sam Erenberg
mementos (Los Angeles 1942), 2009
Watercolor on Arches paper 41 X 29.5 inches

SAM ERENBERG

Sam Erenberg's films, installations, books and paintings have been exhibited throughout the United States, Europe, Asia and Latin America, and are included in numerous collections worldwide including the Museum of Fine Arts, Kunstmuseum Bern, Switzerland; Akademie fuer Sozialarbeit, Bregenz, Austria; Wexford Arts Centre, Wexford, Ireland; Art Metropole Collection, National Gallery of Canada; Smithsonian Library; UCLA Armand Hammer Museum; New Mexico Museum of Art; San Diego Museum of Art; Santa Barbara Museum of Art and the Skirball Cultural Museum among others.

He is a recipient of grants from the Durfee Foundation, the City of Los Angeles COLA Grant and the California Arts Council. Erenberg lives and works in Santa Monica, California.

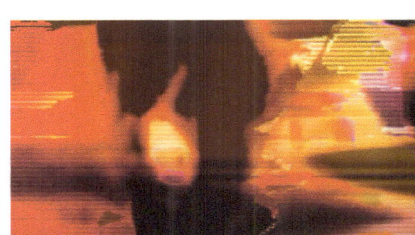

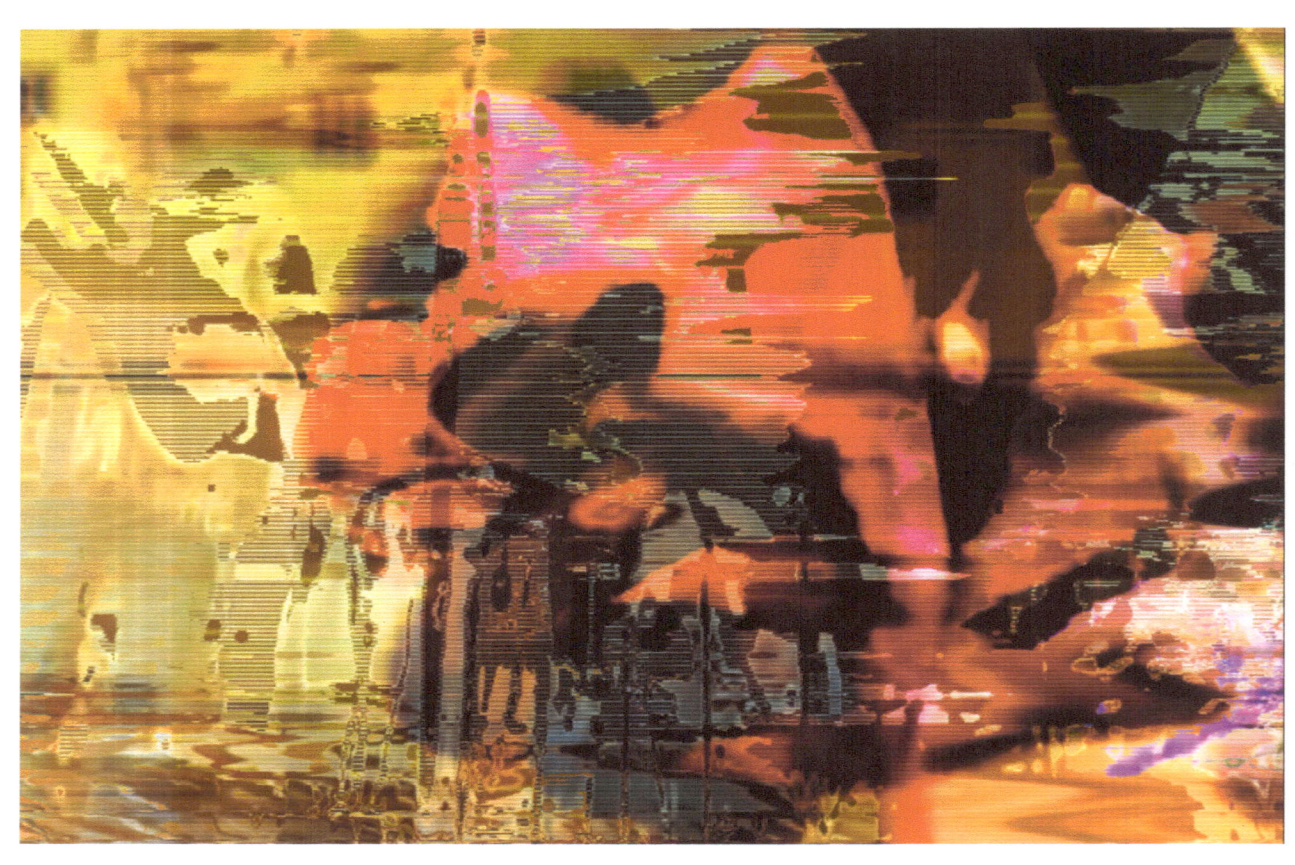

Kio Griffith
Star Spangled Banner 00:06:04, 2014
Ink Jet on Paper, Various Sizes
Original video: 9 minute 11 seconds; Single-Channel Video, 2-Channel Audio

KIO GRIFFITH

Kio Griffith is a Los Angeles-based visual and sound artist, independent curator, graphic designer and producer. He has exhibited work in Japan, Hong Kong, Korea, Turkey, Belgium and the U.S. His work includes drawing, painting, sound, video, performance, electronics, language, sculpture and installation.

He has shown work as a solo artist, in a collaboration, or group locally and internationally at the Los Angeles Municipal Art Gallery, REDCAT, Track 16 Gallery, New Image Art Gallery, Rocket Gallery (Japan), Gallery Lara (Japan), Mathilde Hatzenberger Gallery (Belgium), Moon Gallery (Hong Kong), Busan Film Festival (Korea) ADC Contemporary Art, Eagle Rock Center for the Arts, ResBox, Jaus Gallery, RAID Projects, Giant Robot (GR2) Gallery, Highways Performance Space and was the guest composer for the opening of the Broad Contemporary Art Museum, Los Angeles County Museum of Art.

He has performed visually or musically with Vinny Golia, Ulrich Krieger, Alex Cline, Nels Cline, Mike Watt, Dwight Trible, Miguel Atwood-Ferguson, Dan Morris, Emily Hay, Oguri, Hans Fjellestad, Brad Dutz, Daren Burns, Motoko Honda, Johannes Bergmark, Carmina Escobar, Alan Nakagawa and others.

Griffith has also been recognized by AIGA for design excellence and also garnered recognition from Print's Design Annual and the Society of Illustrators for his work.

Griffith's work is based in his research into the visual and sonic possibilities of the mysteries, myths, and materials embedded within modern life. His compositional process mimics the writing of music and is inspired by the sources of everyday matters of consciousness. In this process, interrelated references of time and space are coordinated into the periphery of mass culture. Generating references from hypermedia and their resonating signals, Griffith's "scores" comprise visual and auditory transcriptions.

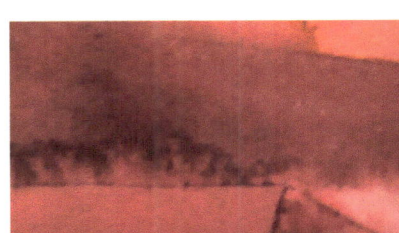

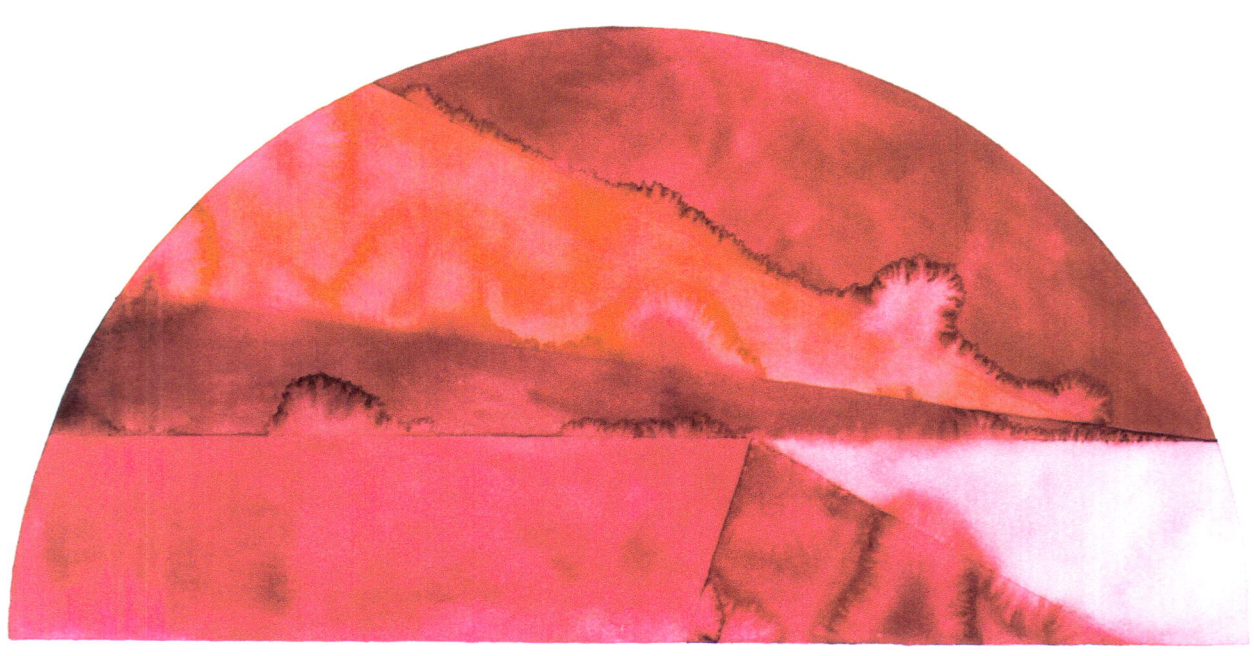

Gloriane Harris
Vermillion Fire, 1980/2014
Watercolor on Arches paper, 18 X 24 inches

GLORIANE HARRIS

Gloriane Harris was born in 1947 in Santa Monica, California. Always living close to the ocean and beaches of Southern California, she has found that the light of the ocean and the beach is like nothing anywhere else. This is the greatest influence on her painting. The four elements always must be present somewhere in her paintings: air, earth, fire, and water.

She earned her MFA from Otis Art Institute. She worked with Nam June Paik and Charlotte Moorman on an historic worldwide satellite broadcast at Documenta 6, in Kassel, Germany. She has taught art at Otis Art Institute, El Camino College, Cerritos College, among several other institutions.

She has exhibited at museums and galleries across the U.S. and Europe, including the Los Angeles County Museum of Art, the Newport Art Museum, and the Los Angeles Design Center, and the Palais de Beaux Arts in Belgium, and has been curated into shows by Peter Frank and John Lees among others. She has appeared in art publications such as Who's Who in American Art and Art in America.

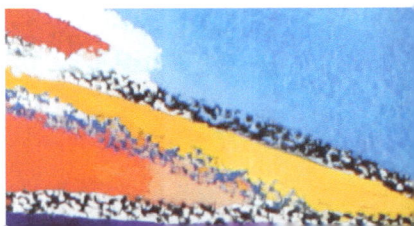

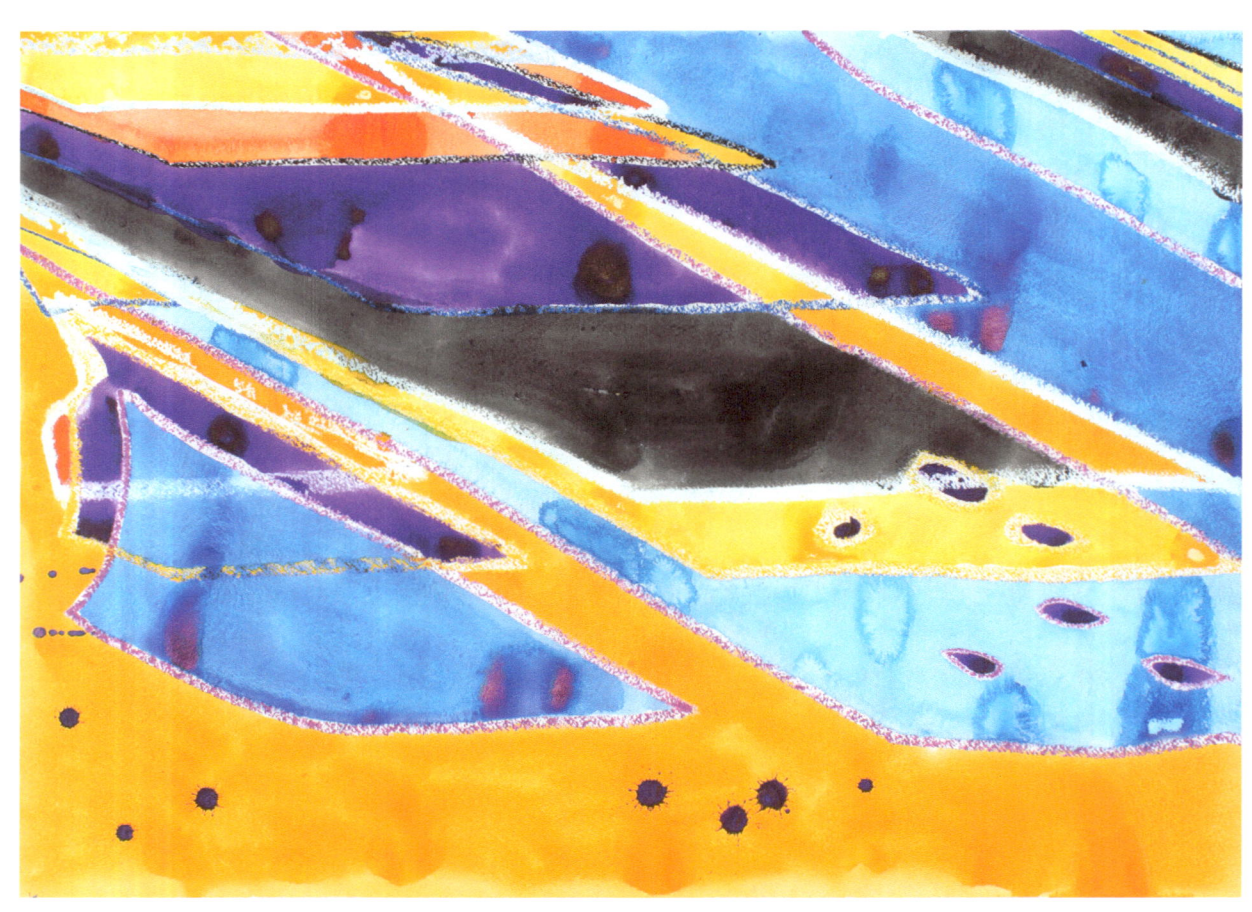

Juri Koll
Windows Cad Yellow Deep I, 2014
Watercolor on paper, 30 X 22.5 inches

JURI KOLL

Juri Koll's paintings, films, and photographs have been exhibited in galleries across the U.S. since the late 1970's. . After graduating from California Institute of the Arts, Koll produced the first Art/World documentaries from 1990-1995. He traveled across the U.S. to work with major curators in their museums and galleries, such as the Metropolitan Museum of Art in New York City. The National Gallery in Washington, DC, the Los Angeles County Museum of Art in Los Angeles, and the Museum of Modern Art in San Francisco. His subjects included world famous and infamous artists and curators from the Renaissance period to the present.

Koll's first documentary, In The Steel: A Portrait of Mark di Suvero, (1991), was accepted into the Archives of American Art at the Smithsonian Institution.

Koll is a member of the Directors Guild of America. He has produced and/or directed over 60 films, both fiction and documentaries. His films have screened all over the world, in over 70 festivals, including Cannes, the Cork International Film Festival, the Australian International Film Festival, and won many awards. He recently directed and screened a a feature documentary about artist Lisa Adams to critical acclaim in Los Angeles.

Koll directs and curates exhibitions for the Venice Institute of Contemporary Art ViCA recently helped sponsor the Trans Angeles exhibition curated by Peter Frank at the Wilhelm-Morgner-Haus in Soest, Germany, and will be producing a feature documentary about the traveling show.

Juri Koll writes articles on the art world for publications such as the Huffington Post and Fabrik and has been published in the New York Times.

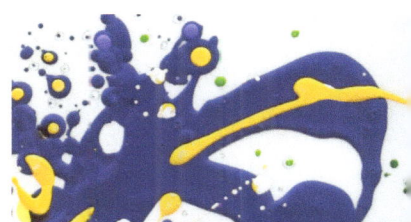

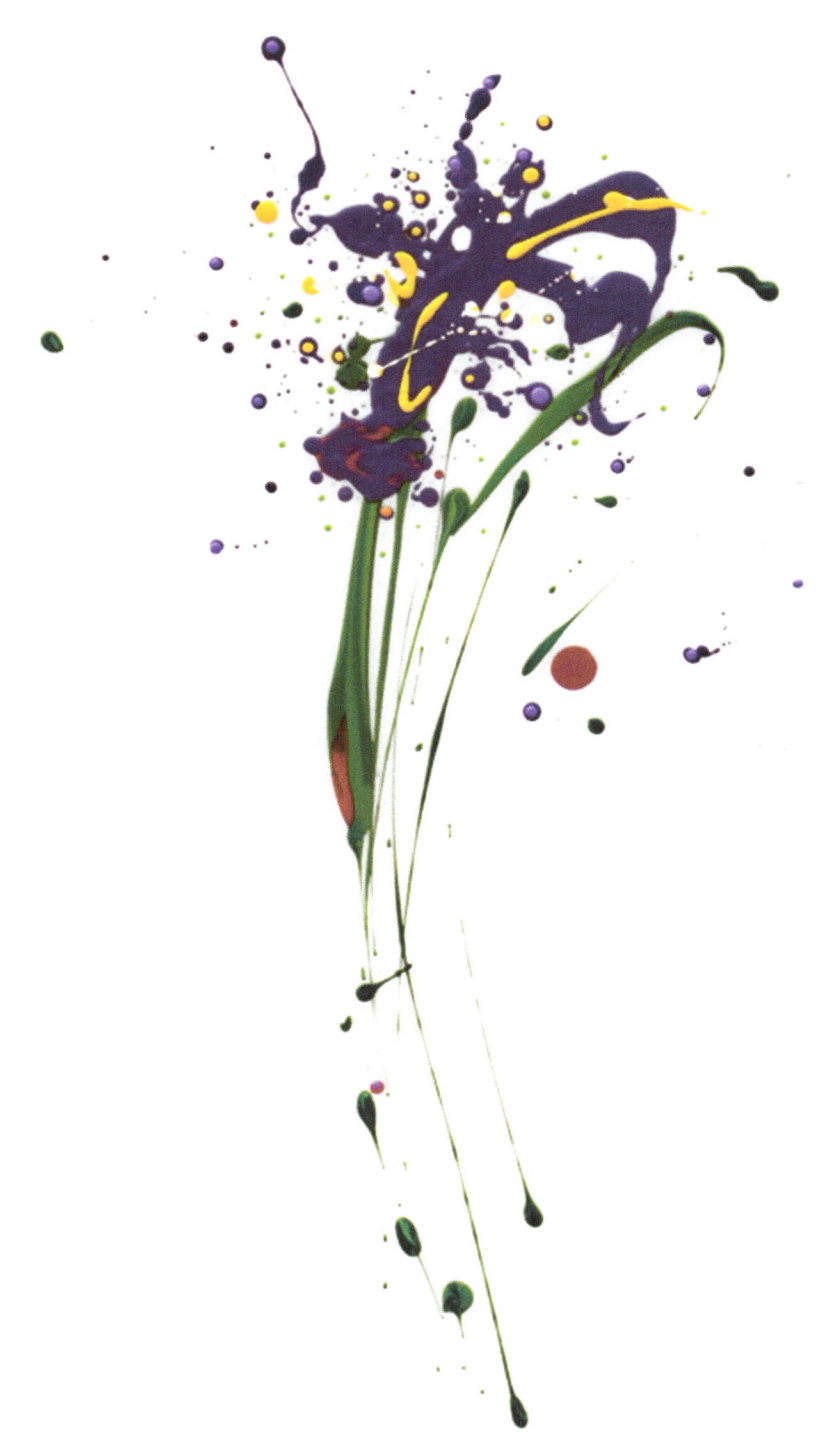

Barbara Kolo
Flora VIII, 2014
Acrylic Paint on Drafting Film, 24 X 18 inches

BARBARA KOLO

Barbara Kolo was born and educated in New York. Having developed an appreciation for art from an early age, her interest in drawing and painting lead her to attend the High School of Art and Design, followed by the School of Visual Arts. She received her BFA from SVA.

During the 1980's Barbara built a career as an award-winning art director in creative advertising for films and television. As an independent freelance art director she worked directly with major film studios and design studios specializing in film advertising. In 1991, she accepted the position of Director of Print Advertising at Universal Studios.

Barbara's early interest in drawing and painting had never diminished. During the early '90's, she followed the urge to develop her own personal artistic voice and began create her own works. Her drawings were soon being included in local and national group shows. The artist moved to Paris, France in 2000. She rented an art studio by La Bastille, and participated in "Genie de la Bastille" an event similar to the Venice Art Walk in California. Her paintings were part of several group exhibitions in France including one at the Palais des Art in Marseilles. In 2003, the couple returned to Santa Monica and Kolo re-established herself in the local art community.

Barbara's work is represented by Jan Kossen Contemporary in Basel, Switzerland, Fresh Paint Art Advisors as well as Artspace Warehouse in Los Angeles. She is a member of the Los Angeles Art Association. Recently, Rebecca Wilson, director at Saatchi Gallery, London has included Kolo's work in many collections for Saatchi Online, and Artslant the #1 Contemporary Art Network placed Barbara Kolo on their Showcase Watchlist of emerging artists. Her work can be found in public institutions and private collections internationally.

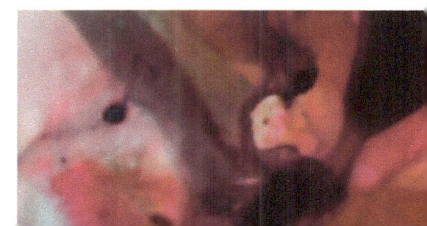

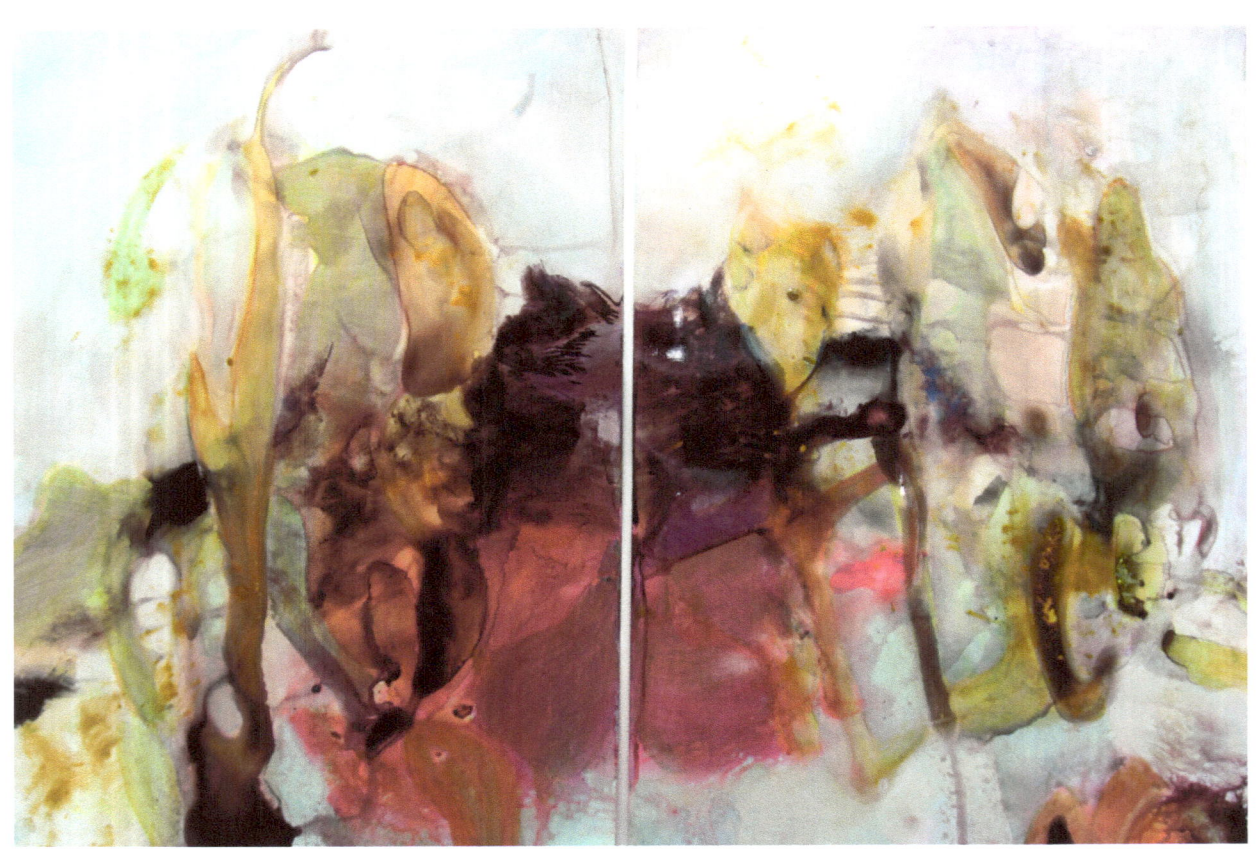

KuBO
HK S2, 2014
Dyptichkon, Multi-layered pigment on paper, 21.5 X 31.5 inches

KuBO

KuBO, born in 1962, has lived and worked in Los Angeles, Hong Kong, and Sweden as well as his native Germany for the past several years, as much to accommodate his international business work as to stimulate his artwork. His art-making encompasses painting, sculpture, photography, and combinations thereof, and capitalizes on his extensive employment of and research into pigments, inks, and coatings. This research in turn has been spurred by his longtime commitment to worldwide ecological practice, and his experience with such materials allows him to give a peculiar luster to the surfaces of his images and objects. Before settling in Hong Kong KuBO lived and worked in several other Asian cities, most notably Istanbul. The nom de plume "KuBO" comes in part from the Cantonese term referring to a broken but repaired vessel, a metaphor for reconciliation after a period of dispute.

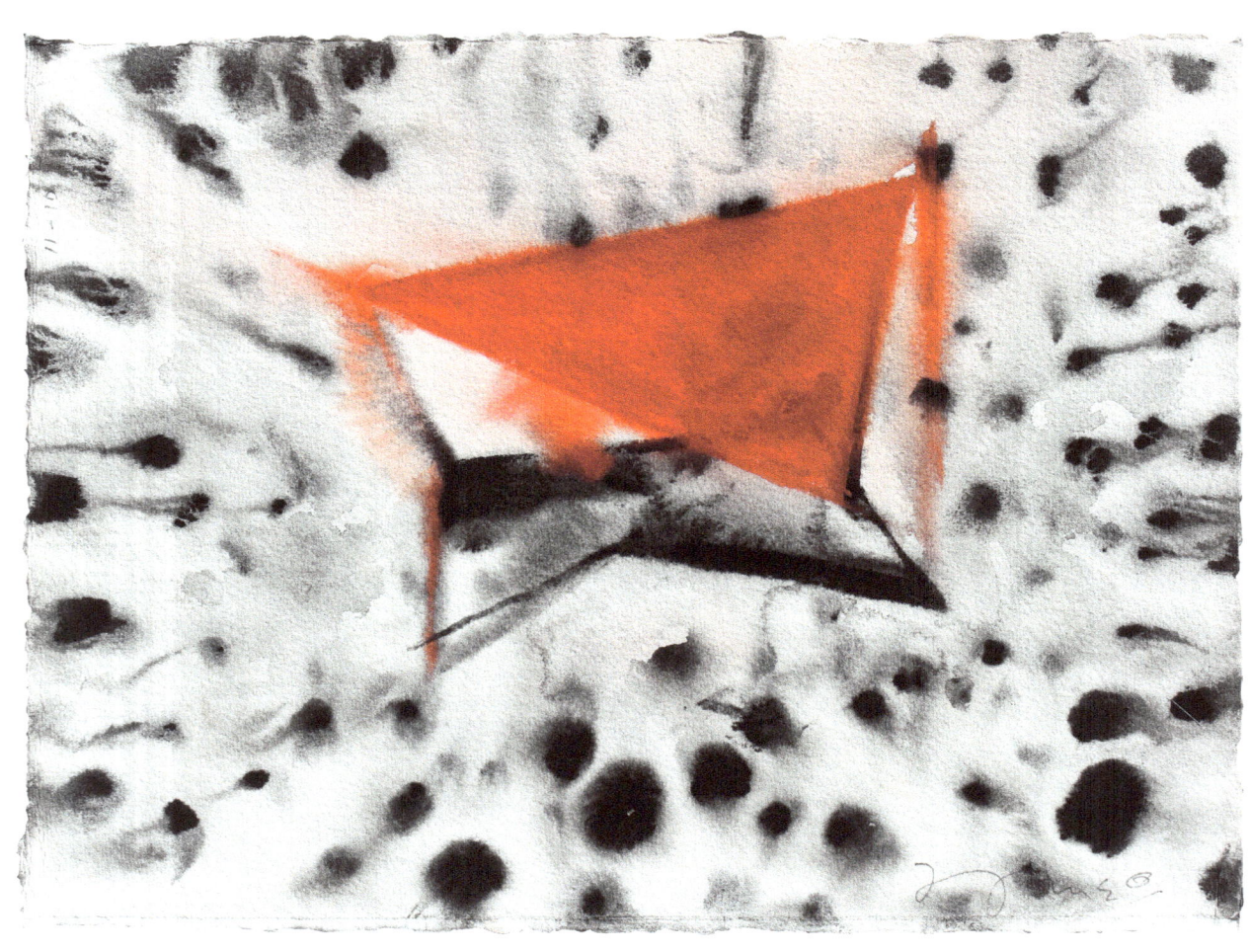

Jayme Odgers
Indeterminate Outcome #2, 2010
Watercolor on 300# Arches rough paper, 11 x 15 inches

JAYME ODGERS

Jayme Odgers is a painter and graphic designer. With a B.A. from Art Center College of Design in Pasadena, California, Odgers is the recipient of numerous awards including a Fulbright Scholarship to Switzerland and over one hundred awards of excellence in graphic design. He was also selected to create an official poster for the 1984 XXIIIrd Olympiad held in Los Angeles along with such distinguished artists as David Hockney, Robert Rauschenberg, Roy Lichtenstein, Jonathan Borofsky, and John Baldessari.

Odgers has taught at many renowned art departments in the Los Angeles area including Art Center College of Design, California Institute of the Arts and Otis College of Art and Design.

Odgers has completed a public art commission designing two water fountains for the Metropolitan Water District's Headquarters Building at Union Station in downtown Los Angeles.

Numerous books and articles have included Odgers' work, most significantly The 20th Century Poster. Design of the Avant Garde (Abbeville Press, New York), POSTMODERISM, Style and Subversion 1970 -1990 at the Victoria & Albert Museum in London in 2012. His work is included in the latest Dictionary of Graphic Design and Designer by Thames & Hudson and Megg's History of Graphic Design.

His work has been exhibited at the Brooklyn Museum, The San Francisco Museum of Art, Arco Center for the Visual Arts,The Albright Knox Museum and the Montreal Museum of Fine Arts, The Victoria & Albert Museum, London, England, with inclusion in the permanent collections of the Smithsonian's Cooper-Hewitt Museum in NewYork City and The White House in Washington, D.C.

Jayme Odgers lives and works in downtown Los Angeles.

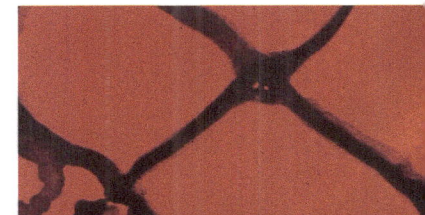

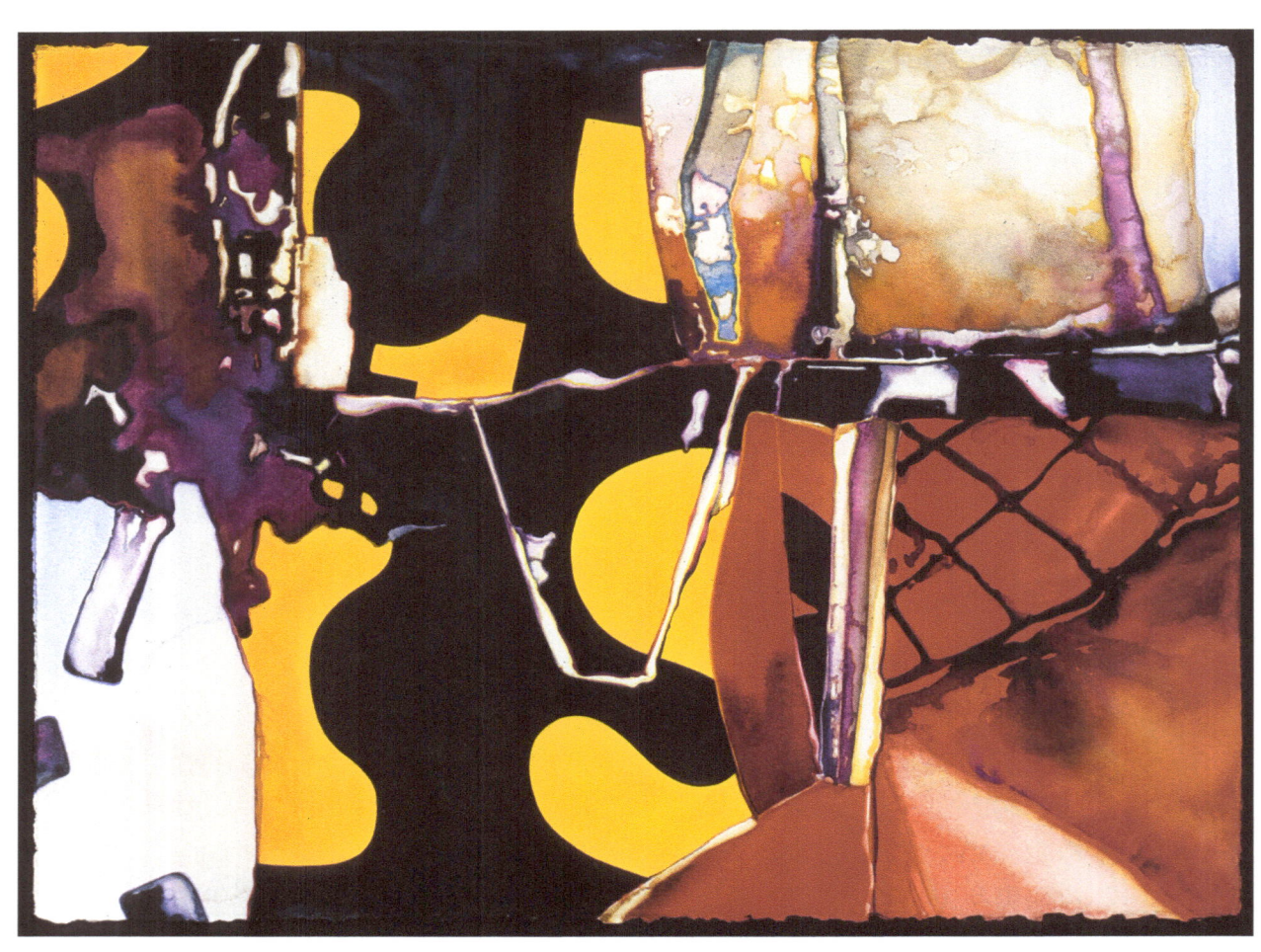

Kirk Pedersen
Dior, 2011
Watercolor on Arches paper, 22 X 30 inches

KIRK PEDERSEN

Kirk Pedersen received graduate degrees from San Francisco State University and Claremont Graduate University. He has exhibited extensively at major galleries, art fairs and museums throughout the United States, Germany, Switzerland, and China, including the Today Art Museum in Beijing and Shanghai's Duolun Museum of Modern Art. Since 1997 Pedersen has served as professor of painting and drawing at Mt. San Antonio College outside Los Angeles.

Traveling to Hong Kong, Bangkok, Tokyo, Taipei, Kuala Lumpur, and many other cities in Asia to capture what he calls Urban Asia, Pedersen examines the seemingly ordinary stuff of life-sidewalks, curbs, markets, alleys-and, through his eye for rhythm, color, and synchronicity, reveals new truths about the world around us. He works in various painting, paper, and photographic media.

Pedersen launched ZERO+ Publishing in January 2009. The imprint, which specializes in monographic publications, focuses on street and Pop Surrealist artists from Los Angeles. To date the imprint has published almost 30 unique titles, many of them including deluxe limited editions designed by the artists in concert with Pedersen.

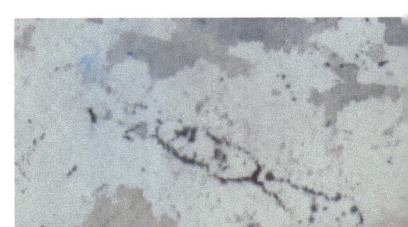

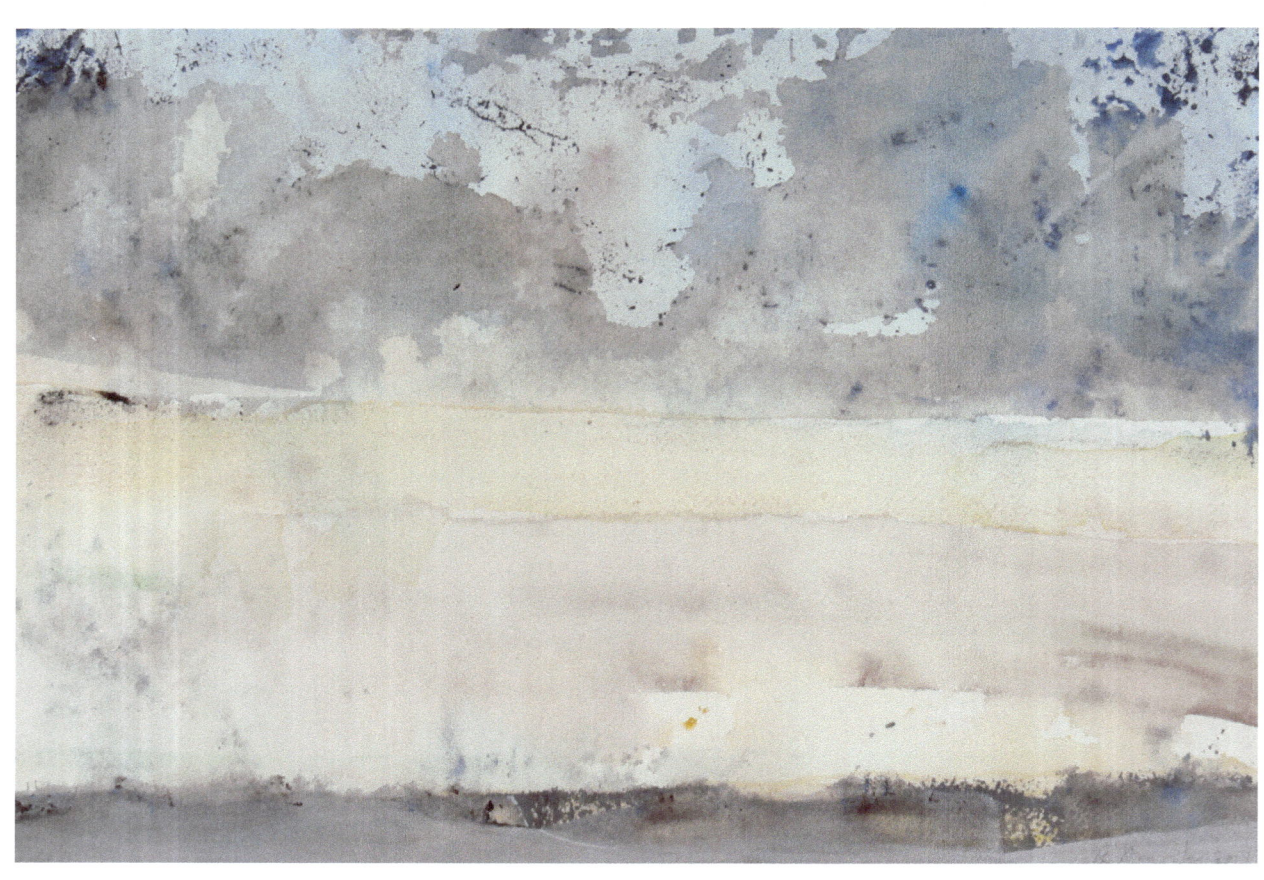

Kate Register
Landing, 2013
Watercolor/Acrylic on paper, 9 X 13 inches

KATE REGISTER

Born in Greenwich, Connecticut, Kate Register received her BFA from Rhode Island School of Design. Register was accepted and joined the European Honors Program in Rome. She attended The Cooper Union School of Art in NY in 1988. Register taught art at The Buxton School in Williamstown, Massachusetts. She also taught art at First Pres. in Santa Monica, California. Register mentored under Ken Price and was his art assistant in Venice, California. A solo trip around the world was documented with watercolors, collage, photography and extensively illustrated journals. This trip took Register to remote villages in Vietnam, the Lofoten Islands of Norway, a camel safari in the Thar Desert of India and the mountains of Ubud, Indonesia to name just a few of Register's destinations. In 1997-98 Register travelled to over 21 countries and has continued to travel; incorporating landscapes imprinted on her soul into paintings.

Living currently in Santa Monica, Kate Register comes from a legacy of artists. Her father is John Register (1940-1996) the well-known California realist painter.

Kate Register was accepted and attended the 2013 art residency program in Greece at the The Skopelos Art Foundation.

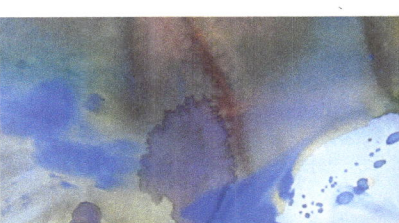

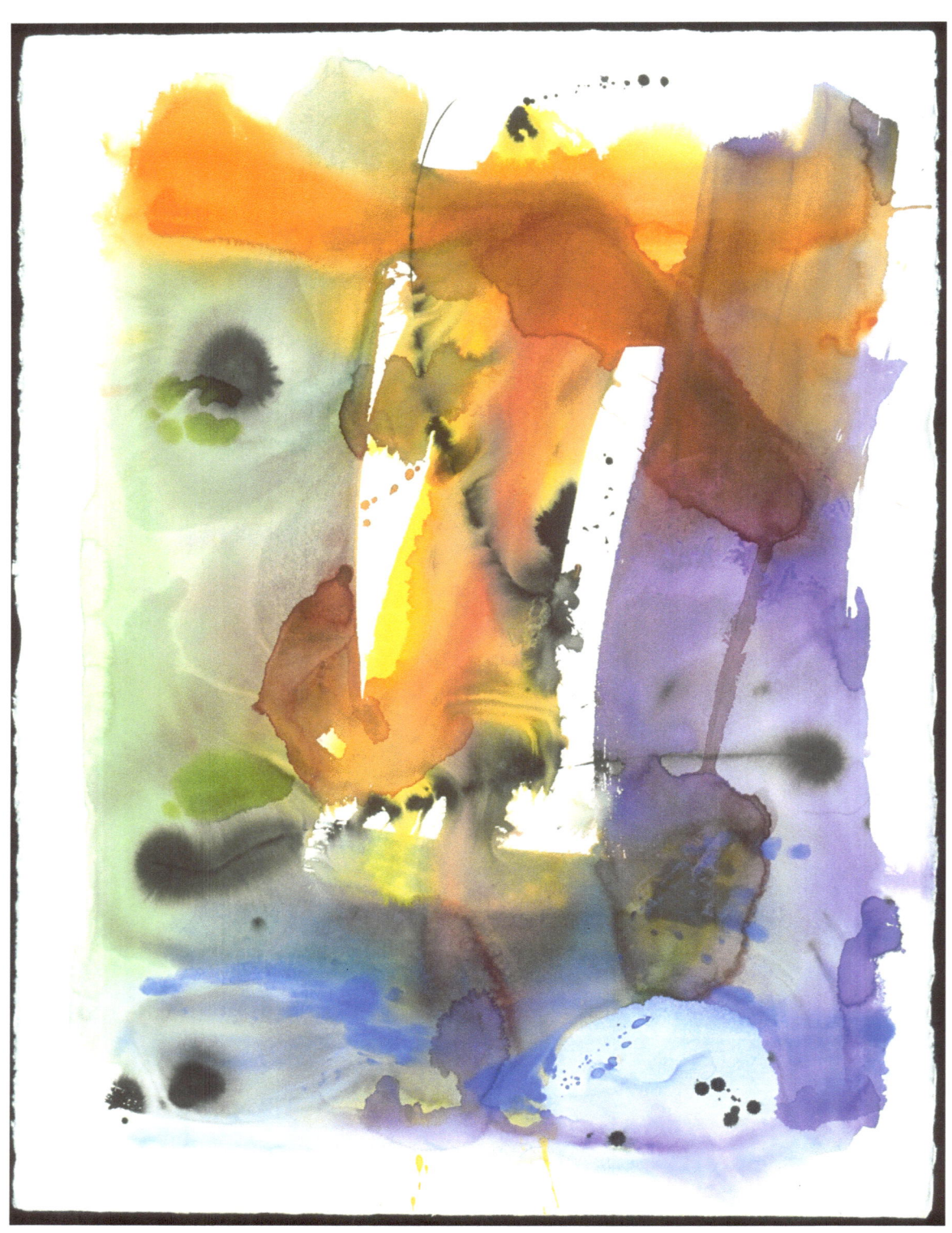

Karrie Ross
Symbol, 1998
Watercolor on Arches paper, 30 X 22 inches

KARRIE ROSS

Born and raised in Los Angeles, California, Karrie Ross discovered her passion for art at an early age inspired by a friend-of-the-family who painted watercolors and was part of the Laguna Beach, CA art scene of the 1950s. Ross then grew into an appreciation of concept, quality, form; a love of line, color, and construction from Disney cartoons and the genius of Saul Bass design to historical artists such as Miro, Matisse, Picasso, Dali, Duchamp, Man Ray and more. In the 1980s (and might be considered part of the Pacific Standard Time era of artists) when she started showing at venues in and around Los Angeles, her purpose was to be seen, learn to talk about her art and create a collectors base.

In the mid-1990s, a company that worked with the decorative industry approached her to be one of their gallery artists. Her paintings were sold to, and placed around the world in hotels, commercial, residential, and retail venues for the next 15 years.

Ross explores the concepts of energy creation, science, participation, discontectedness, and being seen, as the underlying influences of her art. Metaphorical and most-times, whimsical representations that create a `safe' place for the viewer to experience a flow, the growing of energy in balance, a never ending spiral momentum of up and out, encouraging their connection from interaction with the artwork, discovering that they are part of a bigger whole.

She works in both watercolor and oil as they seem "more alive" to her as well as pen & ink or pencil for her never-ending fascination with doodling.

In the end, Ross is about the seeing of oneself and the knowing of ones personal energy. Her work is her on going creative exploration of what makes her who she is...each line, color or stroke she makes.

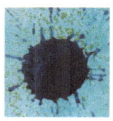

Venice Institute of Contemporary Art
Mission Statement

The Venice Institute of Contemporary Art (ViCA) is a non-profit arts organization devoted to identifying and sustaining the history and essence of one of the most important centers of American artistic activity.

ViCA protects, preserves, and promotes the values of independent artistic expression that have driven the force of creativity in Venice since the founding of the city in 1905.

Through its exhibitions, events, research facilities, and education curriculum, ViCA will celebrate the art, culture and community that Venice Beach has provided to Southern California and the world at large. This marks the beginning of a concerted effort to comprehend the world art community through the lens of Venice.

Since its inception ViCA has and will continue to create important events and exhibitions taking place in galleries and specialized spaces as it raises funds for a permanent home.

Sam Francis Foundation Mission Statement

Building on Sam Francis's creative legacy, the Sam Francis Foundation is dedicated to the transformative power of art as a force for change. We are committed to advancing a greater understanding of Sam Francis's art and ideas through programs and activities designed to educate, inform, and catalyze new thinking about the importance of creativity in society.

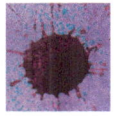

www.ingramcontent.com/pod-product-compliance
Lightning Source LLC
Chambersburg PA
CBHW050407180526
45159CB00005B/2183